LIGHT DEVOTIONS FOR HAPPY CHRISTIANS

The Spanking Machine & Other Stories
From the Good Old Days

Wayne Taylor

Pacific Press® Publishing Association
Nampa, Idaho
Oshawa, Ontario, Canada

Edited by B. Russell Holt
Designed by Dennis Ferree
Cover art by Carol Strebel

Copyright © 2000 by
Pacific Press® Publishing Association
Printed in the United States of America
All Rights Reserved

ISBN 0-8163-1784-4

00 01 02 03 04 • 5 4 3 2 1

CONTENTS

INTRODUCTION

Why are we here? This mystery has baffled the great philosophers all through the ages. Without the solid anchor point of eternity, these wise people have operated at a severe disadvantage in attempting to answer that question.

My somewhat simple mind has the answer. We are here on this earth to learn lessons that will prepare us for the infinity of eternity. However you measure it, the length of our lives on this earth is minuscule compared to eternity. The spiritual lessons we need to learn may be totally serious, but sometimes we glean them from some rather hilarious bloopers and blunders in which we are the main actors. So many times I've found myself getting into a colossal mess that turns out to be downright funny in retrospect. Does God allow these incidents just to provide us with meaningless humorous interludes? Are true spiritual lessons contained only in somber events?

I don't think so. I believe that "*all* things work together for good to them that love God" (Romans 8:28, KJV, emphasis supplied). "All things" include experiences that are comical. So I've learned to laugh heartily at myself for the last fiasco I've pulled; but I've also learned to dig deeply to extract the lessons from those experiences—lessons that help prepare me for eternity.

This book is a collection of stories that happened to me during my "growing up" years—years that spanned elementary school, academy, college, and two post-college years spent as an Army draftee. Although some of the stories are about events from my childhood, this is not a book of stories for children. Rather, it's a book that I hope will cause adults to look back, laugh, and then take a serious look at the lessons found in these experiences and the implications for their own lives.

Despite accusations to the contrary, the stories are all true! Names of the people involved (other than my own) are not. I've changed names to protect a few innocent people and many more whose innocence may be somewhat suspect. Most place names are correct, but again, I've changed a few when the specific locale might be too much of a tip-off to the identity of an individual.

Finally, this book would not exist if it were not for Frank Dupper. Before his retirement, Frank was president of Adventist Health, with headquarters in Roseville, California. Adventist Health is one of eight regional Seventh-day Adventist healthcare systems that collectively own my organization, Healthcare Excess Liability Management Cooperative, Inc. Frank was my board chairman. As such, he was my boss; he is also my long-time friend.

Wearing the "friend hat," Frank had urged me for years to compile these stories into a book. I gave him a lot of positive lip service based on good intentions, but no action. Finally he put on his "boss hat" to underscore his urging. That method of "explaining the benefits" gave me the necessary kick in the pants to actually do something about it and produce the book I really wanted to write all along.

Thanks, Frank. I needed that!

CHAPTER 1

Mr. Smith and the Spanking Machine

The crucial moment had arrived. I was about to embark upon an ambitious venture that would alter my life and redirect my future. I was six years old, and it was my first day of school.

Determined to be brave, but holding tightly to my mother's hand, I approached the school building. It was a massive edifice, looming two full stories into the sky. Yet it was dominated by an even loftier front tower that pierced the clouds at the dizzy height of three stories.

Going directly to the first-grade room, my mother introduced me to my teacher, Miss Carlson. Then Mother said a quick Goodbye and left.

There I was, left to face this brave new world alone. What was school all about? What was in store? Oh, I had heard rumors from other kids, but nothing I wanted to believe. I needed answers, fast!

Obviously, those answers could not come from my fellow first-graders. They were all just as new and green as I was. Miss Carlson was a grown-up, so anything she said could not be trusted.

Answers began to unfold, however, when I was introduced to the first element of the curriculum that actually made sense to me. This was an event known as recess. The first grade and the second grade had recess together. Out on the playground, I was approached by another boy.

"Hi," he said, "my name is Pete. I'm a second-grader."

This was a momentous occasion. Here I was, a lowly first-grader, being approached by an exalted, worldly-wise second-grader. He had been over the road before. He could speak from the wealth of his vast storehouse of experience. Clearly, he had all the answers that I had been needing. What an opportunity for information! My questions came pouring out, and Pete was most gracious in his willingness to respond.

In the midst of the Q & A session, I interrupted Pete to ask, "Who is that man at the other end of the schoolyard?"

Pete's countenance clouded. His voice lowered. "That's Mr. Smith," he replied. "He's the principal."

"What's a principal?" I asked. "What does a principal do? What is his job?"

Pete motioned me closer. I could sense that he was about to lay something heavy on me. In solemn, measured tones, he said, "A principal's job is to spank kids."

I gasped!

"And," he continued, "Mr. Smith hangs out in a room on the second floor of the tower, called the office."

"What's an office?" I inquired.

Pete bluntly answered, "An office is a room for spanking kids. And do you know what Mr. Smith has in that office?"

"No . . . what?" I sensed something even more ominous was coming.

"A spanking machine," Pete gravely answered in his most gripping tones.

A spanking machine! My mind recoiled with horror! Chills ran up and down my spine. But Pete continued relentlessly, "You'd better stay away from Mr. Smith because all he does all day is go around grabbing kids to put into his spanking machine. Especially keep away from the door to the office because Mr. Smith might open it, snatch you up, and put you into the spanking machine."

"Has he ever put you into the spanking machine?" I asked.

"No, I stay out of his way."

"Then how do you know there really is a spanking machine?" I probed.

"I've seen it with my own eyes," he retorted, "and seeing is believing."

Back in the classroom, I quickly learned that other first grade colleagues had also been approached by concerned second-graders bearing the solemn warning message about Mr. Smith, the office, and the spanking machine. With missionary zeal, the second-graders had fanned out across the playground, each bearing testimony in one-on-one witnessing, proclaiming the urgent alarm.

The first Wednesday brought us closer to the peril. Miss Carlson explained that each Wednesday all the students in all grades were to go upstairs to the auditorium for chapel. We lined up in the hallway outside our classroom door. (The first thing Miss Carlson had taught us was to line up. We formed a line for everything we did. I was convinced that lining up must be the fundamental cornerstone of education.)

Our door was near the foot of the stairs leading up to a landing. The stairs then turned for the last few steps up to the auditorium level. As we stood there in line and looked up the stairs, our hearts froze.

There, at the top of that first landing, was the door to the dreaded chamber of horrors, the OFFICE!

A wave of panic reverberated through the line of first-graders. At least the door to the office was closed, but Mr. Smith might be lurking behind it. Miss Carlson, apparently not noticing our fear, gave the order to move. The line didn't budge.

In firmer tones, she again gave the order. No movement.

After various types of persuasion, from threats to rewards, the line began to slowly make its way up the steps. Near the landing, each first grader stopped, made a mad dash past the office door, and then proceeded up the final steps.

Safely in our seats in the auditorium, we did a quick check on our companions. Not one had fallen victim to Mr. Smith and the spanking machine.

Many Wednesdays lay ahead, however, and on each one, the ritual played itself out again. Interestingly, Mr. Smith never opened the door to grab a first grader as fodder for his spanking machine.

No one would openly admit it, but faith in the spanking-machine doctrine was showing some signs of unraveling. A few bold first-graders, instead of dashing past the office door, actually began to flirt with danger by defiantly dancing across the landing. Some people seem to tempt disaster in order to impress others.

Then one Wednesday, it happened. As we lined up at the foot of the stairs, we looked up and saw something we had never seen before.

The office door was open. THE OFFICE DOOR WAS OPEN!

This sobered even the most courageously flippant first-grader. A trepidation reminiscent of the first Wednesday of the school year gripped the entire class. A newly cautious group of first-graders gingerly ascended the stairs. At the landing, each one sped past the door with unprecedented haste.

After I completed my own sprint past the open door and started up the final steps, curiosity overtook me. Like Lot's wife, I looked back into the office to quickly check out its contents. There was a desk. There was a typewriter. There were some chairs. But there, over against the wall, there it was!

Big, black, and forbidding—the SPANKING MACHINE!

I saw it! I saw it with my own eyes! And seeing is believing!

At the first opportunity, we first—graders debriefed each other. Virtually every one had looked back, and each had seen the spanking machine with his or her own eyes. There was no doubt now. Pete and the other second-graders had been vindicated. How could we have ever doubted their warning admonition?

No one wavered in their faith in the spanking-machine message again. Theory had become indisputable fact!

The school year passed. Mr. Smith had not grabbed a single first-grader to put into the spanking machine. We credited these exemplary results to our renewed caution.

Summer vacation came and went too quickly. We soon found ourselves trudging back to school. This time, however, we did not come to school as lowly, intimidated first-graders. We came as seasoned, all-knowing second-graders.

At the first recess of the school year, we instinctively took up the torch to spread the alarm to the new unsuspecting first-graders. We saturated the playground with our personal testimony, proclaiming the message of Mr. Smith and the spanking machine.

That school year passed, too, but when we returned as third graders, we were too advanced and mature to take recess with the juveniles in the first and second grades. Not to worry. The new crop of second-graders performed admirably as they carried on the crusade to indoctrinate the new crop of first-graders.

And so it went, year after year.

It was several years after this before three great truths began to dawn on me.

Great Truth Number One: A principal has other duties besides spanking kids.

Great Truth Number Two: Mr. Smith was actually a very kind man and in no way a brutal child abuser.

Great Truth Number Three: A mimeograph machine is not a spanking machine.

For those too young to remember the primitive world that existed before the widespread availability of the photocopy machine, a bit of explanation may be in order. Mimeograph machines were a school's most common means of duplicating written materials or tests. To mimeograph an item, a page called a "master" must be prepared. The master resembled a piece of paper coated with a somewhat dry, gummy substance. The master could be prepared longhand with a stylus, but usually a typewriter was used.

The master was then wrapped around the drum of the mimeograph machine, and ink was forced through these perforations. Each turn of the drum would reproduce the image of the master on another sheet of paper.

Yes, we had seen something. We had seen it with our own eyes, but we had not seen the full picture. If we had, we would have known that what we saw was not a spanking machine. Instead, it was a device to reproduce the image of a master.

Even worse, we had maligned the character of a very good man, Mr. Smith.

Perhaps the lower-grade students, who believed and perpetuated the story, behaved better than they would have it they had not been afraid of Mr. Smith and the spanking machine. If behavior is the only thing that counts, then the spanking-machine story had some justification.

On the other hand, if anything else matters— such as truth or the avoidance of character assassination—then the spanking-machine story was an abomination.

The Bible gives us the great commission in several places, but nowhere more succinctly than Mark 16:15. "Go into all the world and preach the gospel to the whole creation" (RSV). Anyone with exposure to any Christian church knows that the word "gospel" means "good news." Not to insult anyone's intelligence, but "good" is not "bad." The two words are not only opposites, they are mutually exclusive. Good news (the gospel) cannot be bad news. We are told to preach the good news. We have been given an overwhelming amount of good news, the best news in the universe, the message of hope, redemption, and salvation.

Why then do we prefer to spread bad news? If second-graders had realized that Mr. Smith was a good man and that the machine in the office was a mimeograph machine, how much enthusiasm would they have shown in sharing that news? It is a basic premise of journalism that bad news sells more newspapers than good news.

Why are we more prone to give "the warning message" (bad news) than "the message of hope" (good news)? In the Bible, the good news far outweighs the bad news. Is it easier to scare people into accepting Christ by picturing God as some celestial Mr. Smith who gets His jollies by putting people into some version of a spanking machine?

Why don't we proclaim a positive message—that God is calling us into the supreme joy of a closer relationship with Him? This is good news. This is truth. This represents the character of God correctly. This brings about behavior change based on the right reason.

Some have said, "Better to scare people into the church than for them not to come in at all."

Really? Are you sure? During the Inquisition, the established religion tortured dissenters, trying to force them to recant. The leaders attempted to justify their actions by saying, "It is better for people to be tortured so that they will not burn in eternal hell fire."

Is there a moral difference between torturing people to force them to behave and frightening them to force them to behave?

Perhaps, but only if you believe that behavior is the only thing that counts. The lower-grades were frightened into behaving correctly around Mr. Smith, but only because they had been deceived about his character. Should we malign God's character by picturing him as cruel and vicious in order to intimidate people into behavioral change? If behavioral change is motivated by fear instead of love, does it count for anything?

"Now just a minute," you may be saying, "are you suggesting that God will not punish the wicked?"

Not at all and in no way. Everyone should be told that the Bible clearly teaches that God will destroy unrepentant sinners. However, they need to know that He does it with tears in His eyes. "Say to them, 'As surely as I live, declares the sovereign Lord, I take no pleasure in the death of the wicked, but rather that they turn from their ways and live. Turn! Turn from your evil ways! Why will you die, O house of Israel?'" (Ezekiel 33:11, NIV).

God is not a sadistic, bloodthirsty Mr. Smith. He loves all the creatures of His hand with an inexhaustible love. Destroying those who ultimately choose to reject His love brings no pleasure to Him. He does reluctantly destroy, but He has no spanking-machine mentality.

"What?" you say, "Of course there is a spanking machine. It is in the Bible. I have seen it. I have seen it with my own eyes, and seeing is believing. Check out the third angel's message in Revelation 14:9-11."

And the third angel followed them, saying with a loud voice, If any man worship the beast and his image and receive his mark in his forehead, or in his hand, the same shall drink of the wine of the wrath of God which is poured out without mixture into the cup of his indignation; and he shall be tormented with fire and brimstone in the presence of the holy angels, and in the presence of the Lamb!

And the smoke of their torment ascendeth up for ever and ever: and they have no rest day nor night, who worship the beast and his image, and whosoever receiveth the mark of his name. (KJV)

"There it is—the third angel's message that we are to give to the world! No message of hope there—nothing but a warning message. Clearly, this is a spanking machine. I have seen it with my own eyes, and seeing is believing!"

True, seeing is believing—if you see the whole picture. Also true, you saw something in Revelation 14:9-11 that may have looked like a spanking machine.

But there the truth ends unless you are willing to bring the rest of the picture into focus and include the twelfth verse which is also part of the third angel's message:

> Here is the patience of the saints: here are they that keep the commandments of God, and the faith of Jesus (KJV).

Only when you see the full picture do you realize that what you thought was a spanking machine is not a spanking machine at all.

Instead, it is a device to reproduce the image of the Master.

Forging Ahead

The first two of the three R's gave me no problem in school. Unfortunately, the same was not true of the third. Actually, my introduction to arithmetic was simple enough—one number added to another using a plus symbol.

Even in the second grade when I was taught to subtract one number from another using a minus sign, I could still grasp the concept, albeit with some difficulty.

The third grade ushered in what had to be the highest and most complex mathematical process ever devised by the human mind. The plus sign had fallen part way over on its side to form a symbol akin to the letter x. This was the times sign; this was multiplication; this was the outer limit of all conceivable mathematical computation. I struggled to learn the multiplication tables, zero through ten. Only intense commitment to memory brought me through. At least I now knew that arithmetic could not get any more complicated than that.

I was wrong. With my promotion to the fourth grade, I landed squarely in the middle of multiplying multiple digit numbers. Multiplying a multiple digit number by a single digit number was bad enough, but when we hit multiplying multiple digits by multiple digits, I experienced brain overload.

The answers were in the back of the book. The teachers didn't tell us this fact, and they seemed to think we didn't know it. How blind could they be? The answers in the back of the book became my favorite homework companion, although they were rather useless for classroom tests.

Multiplication of multiple numbers by multiple numbers changed my whole approach to homework. The answers given in the back of the book were only the bottom line numbers. They did not show the intermediate two or three rows of multiplication results laid out at an angle which had to be all added to come up with the bottom line total.

My fourth grade teacher was Miss Morris. She was taking us too fast, that was certain. Because of this, I convinced myself that I was justified in cutting corners just a little bit. My homework methodology was to write the two multi-digit numbers, one above the other, and place a times sign in front of the lower number. Then I would draw a line below the numbers. The next step was to come up with some random numerals of my own devising for the next two or three lines. Finally, I would draw a second line under these numbers and beneath it, copy the answer from the back of the book.

This made the bottom-line number correct even though the preceding computations were not. Surely Miss Morris would not look at the intermediate numbers. Who would care what they were as long as the bottom number was right?

Classroom tests challenged my creativity even more. Not having access to the answers from the back of the book, I had to fill *every* line with random numerals. Nothing multiplied out correctly and nothing added correctly. It was just too much effort to do it right. My arithmetic grade plummeted. Miss Morris tried to help me, but when she left my desk, I would revert back to faking random numbers instead of trying the correct method.

At dismissal time one afternoon, Miss Morris called me up to her desk and handed me a folded note.

"I want you to get your parents to read this," she said. "Then have one of them sign it. Bring it back to me tomorrow."

As soon as I was outside, I read the note. As I suspected, Miss Morris had spilled the beans on me. How could I face my parents? What should I do?

Regrettably, the logical answer seemed all too apparent to me. I would forge the name of one of my parents on the note and bring it back to Miss Morris the next day. No one would ever know the difference.

Which parent's name should I use? When I got home, I located some things that each had written. I then did a critical handwriting analysis to determine which name I should select to forge. My mother's name won out. Her handwriting was smoother flowing which I thought would be easier to emulate. Also, her name was shorter.

Enter the first real problem. The advent of the ball-point pen was still several years in the future. All signatures were supposed to be in ink. That meant a fountain pen. I had never touched a fountain pen. Kids my age used pencils—only pencils. The first introduction to ink pens came in the seventh or eighth grade and then often with disastrous results.

If the point of a fountain pen is touched to paper and not moved, ink will pool up on the paper in a big blot. I was not aware of that. In fact, I was completely uninitiated in any of the elements of fountain pen use, including the need to keep the writing flowing forward at all times. I was also unskilled in the fine art of forgery, regardless of the writing instrument involved.

Despite these handicaps, I confidently took pen in hand, looked at a sample of my mother's signature for a guide, and opened the note to be signed. I touched the point of the pen to the note, then glanced at my mother's signature to see which way to begin writing.

When I looked back at the note, a big pool of blue ink was forming where the pen tip touched it. It continued to expand until I moved the pen along the paper. Each time I hesitated to check my mother's signature, the pool of ink would form again. The thought of lifting the pen off the paper never occurred to me.

I finally realized that the faster I moved the pen across the paper, the less pooling and blotting resulted. However, this caused the handwriting to be even more erratic than before.

Finally, I reached the end of her name. Looking at it, I had to admit that it was the worst handwriting I had ever seen. It was a series of big blotches and blots connected by a jagged meandering line that went all over the place. It didn't even look like a name.

Only at this point did the idea dawn on me that I probably should have done a few trial runs with a blank piece of paper before attempting to write on the note itself. On the other hand, the quality of my handiwork was so poor that I was convinced that no amount of practice could elevate it to the high standards of a professional forger.

It was too late. There was no turning back. The permanent ink could not be erased. I would have to turn in the note to Miss Morris the way it was. Maybe she wouldn't notice it.

The next day, I handed Miss Morris the folded note as soon as I arrived at school. All through the day I expected her to call me up to her desk and ask me about it. But the school day ended, and she let us all leave. She had not said one word to me about the note. As I walked home, I was confident that I had gotten away with it.

That evening, when both of my parents were home, I realized that teachers have other ways of communicating with parents besides sending notes home. The invention of the ball-point pen may not have occurred yet, but the invention of the telephone certainly had. Both Miss Morris and my mother were adept at its use.

My parents sat me down for an extremely uncomfortable conversation about the whole incident. They told me how disappointed they were that I would do such a thing. As uncomfortable as the conversation was, I was about to experience even more discomfort. My father shaved with a straight razor at that time. He had a razor strap, the primary purpose of which was to sharpen his razor each time he shaved.

However, the razor strap had a secondary purpose, that of a tool of discipline. It was rarely used for that purpose, and as I look back, probably not nearly often enough. Yet, it was felt that this occasion warranted it. After the discussion, my father took me to my parents' bedroom. Before the ceremony began, he asked me one question, "Do you understand why I am doing this?"

"Y . . . y . . . y . . . yes," I replied fearfully.

He then took the razor strap and delivered some applied psychology to my seat of learning. It definitely smarted, as it was intended to do, but it stopped far short of inflicting any physical injury, which my father would never do.

The occasion was a memorable one. It left an impression on me, although not a physical impression. I would not soon forget this experience. I returned to school a new person. I buckled down and studied as I knew I should. For the next four or five years, I made almost straight A's, even in the dreaded subject of arithmetic.

A good story of effective discipline? A happy ending for a nine-year-old who had started to go the wrong way?

Yes, but not totally in its intended fashion. There were good results, but the cause-and-effect relationship was not what it appeared to be.

You see, there was never a true meeting of the minds between my parents and myself as to why I was being punished. To any adult, it was obvious that the serious offense in this case was the blatant deceit and betrayal I practiced in attempting to forge my mother's signature and in trying to fool Miss Morris into thinking that my parents had read the note.

Somehow, my young mind didn't work that way. Why should I be punished for such a botched case of forgery? Before I had even finished trying to write my mother's name, I was totally aware that I lacked the requisite talent to pursue a career in forgery. I would never try to forge anyone's name again. I had learned that lesson when I first examined the signature I had written. I didn't need any further reinforcement on the forgery issue.

Even at the tender age of nine, I was fully aware that forgery was wrong, although I wasn't sure exactly where it fit among the Ten Commandments. Yet I was overlooking the fact that the overt act of forgery was not the main moral issue here. The real problem was the covert intent to deceive and betray. What is the merit involved if one discontinues forgery, but continues to deceive?

Actually, I thought I was being punished for making bad grades. My poor grades had been bothering my conscience so much that I overlooked the even more serious breach. I was already on a tremendous guilt trip for cheating on my homework by copying answers from the back of the book, and for being too lazy to even try to compute test problems correctly.

My response to the punishment was to become a conscientious model student. It worked, and it lasted a number of years. I began doing the right thing, but for the wrong reason.

If the story ended here without further comment, one might conclude that I ended up as a born-again good student and non-forger, but an unrepentant deceiver. Actually, I came to grips with the deceit issue shortly thereafter, but I became a backslider from straight A's in my later scholastic experience. The forgery lesson was strong enough to last a lifetime. I never forged again. I never wanted to forge again.

Two lessons come out of this. First, at age nine, I saw sin only in the outward act of forgery, overlooking the fact that the most serious aspect of the sin was in my heart. It was the inward motivation to deceive that caused the outward act to happen.

In the Sermon on the Mount, Jesus discussed the sin relationship of the inward thoughts of anger and hatred, compared with the outward act of murder. In the same context He discussed the sin relationship of the inward thoughts of lust, compared with the outward act of adultery (see Matthew 5). "For as he thinketh in his heart, so is he" (Proverbs 23:7, KJV).

The second lesson to be gleaned from this experience relates to doing the right thing for the wrong reason. When I was young, I thought that the story of Jonah had its happy ending when he was regurgitated onto the beach by whatever form of marine life had swallowed him. Now I know that all of the story up to that point is just prologue. The real story of Jonah begins at the gates of Nineveh.

Jonah conducted the most fruitful evangelistic effort of the entire Old Testament. More than 120,000 were converted in a forty-day campaign. Afterward, Jonah sat pouting outside the city, disappointed because his "beloved" converts were not destroyed! His success had sprung from the wrong motivation.

The Bible is full of stories of people who did the right things for the wrong reasons. Similar stories are still happening today.

Do you do good deeds in order to earn salvation? Right thing—wrong reason? Do good deeds in order to earn salvation, and you lose two ways. You won't earn salvation, and you won't enjoy doing the good deeds.

Instead, first let God give you salvation for free. Then you will enjoy doing the good deeds. You win both ways.

How can you beat that offer?

CHAPTER 3

Seeking New Light

Boarding academy was good for me. I may not have been good for it, but it was good for me. It clearly made me a better student. It caused me to focus on the fact that I was going to become an adult and that I had better prepare for it.

Don't be misled into thinking that such serious thoughts occupied my mind constantly. Boarding academy was a blast, and I enjoyed it to the fullest!

Anyone who has ever attended boarding academy knows that one of the greatest pleasures of academy life is complaining about the rules. Complaining about the rules is more than just a joy— it is a downright obligation, almost a matter of principle.

No one could be a member of the "in" crowd

without frequent vociferous griping about the multitudinous injustices heaped upon the student body by the heartless faculty. The faculty's endless lists of *dos* and *don'ts*—written and unwritten—proved that none of them had ever been young.

Clearly violating the Bill of Rights' prohibition against cruel and unusual punishment, the faculty had devised heinous penalties for the most insignificant misconduct. These retributions were not only severe, they were humiliating.

The most popular rules to complain about were the social rules governing interpersonal conduct between the two genders. These were the cruelest injustices.

Lacking the courage to even ask for more than a very few dates a year, I was certainly not the campus Casanova. Therefore, the social rules had little direct impact on me. However, in order to maintain my status as a member of the "in" group, I had to meet my quota of complaining about the social rules.

Many forms of punishment existed, but two stood out as the most mean-spirited and degrading. "De-socialization" topped the list as the supreme penalty for violating the social rules. When students committed a flagrant transgression, such as holding hands with someone of the opposite sex, they were "de-socialized." This meant that for a specified period of time the guilty parties lost all privileges of walking with, talking to, or sitting next to anyone not of the same gender.

Close on its heels for cruel punishment was the penalty of being "campus bound" for a period of time. This punishment was meted out for crimes other than those of a social nature. For example, leaving campus without permission. A guy could not go off campus without permission, no matter how long his hair grew or how much he needed a haircut. (In those days, getting a haircut was not itself a form of punishment as it later became. Short hair, such as crew cuts and flat tops, was the "in" thing in contrast to the rage for long hair of a later generation).

When my own children were in boarding academy, I did a terminology check with them regarding the terms "de-socialized" and "campus bound." After all, as teenagers, they were obviously better informed about the truly important matters of life than was I as a senior citizen. They responded that while the concepts of "de-socialized" and "campus bound" still thrive today in all their glory, the wording has been modernized to simply "socialed" and "campused." As a postscript to informing me of the proper vernacular in this age of enlightenment, they added the helpful and inspiring comment, "Get with the program, Dad. Have you been hiding under a rock?"

For the sake of my story, however, I will revert to the "King James" terminology of "de-socialized" and "campus bound" that was in vogue in my day.

Although I actively complained about the social rules, the restriction that deep down bothered me most had to do with light—or the lack thereof. Each night at 9:30, the dean would unlock the breaker box and turn off all electricity to the dormitory rooms. The hallway lights stayed on, but our rooms were plunged into darkness.

Plunged into darkness! In this age of light!

Thomas Edison would turn over in his grave! The gravity of this injustice worked its way ever deeper into my innermost being. Oh for a liberator to lift the burden of this heavy despised yoke!

As I looked out upon the figurative horizon, no liberator appeared—no one to free us from this bondage of 9:30 P.M. darkness. Was there no hope?

Gradually, the unthinkable began to emerge in my brain. Could I be the one upon whom this mantle should fall? Could I be the liberator?

"No!" was my first reaction. But my quest for justice could not be stilled. "If not you, then who?" I asked myself.

"But," I mused, "I'm a senior, only two months away from graduation. Why waste my efforts when there is so little time left?"

"Do it for others," I thought. "Leave a noble legacy for generations to come. Become for this academy what Edison has become for the rest of the world. Seek light!"

A plan began to take shape in my mind.

The dean's apartment was in the basement with stairs leading down to it from the end of the first floor hall. The dormitory room at that end of the hall and in front of those stairs had been used by the previous dean as an office. The current dean did not want an office, so the room was again made available for student occupancy.

The previous dean had found that when he turned off the lights to the other dormitory rooms at 9:30, it darkened his makeshift office, rendering it useless for late-night work. Therefore, he had a special line wired into a receptacle in the room's closet to provide all-night electricity. With the changing of the deans, the faculty apparently overlooked the existence of the all-night plug. You can bet that the guys in the dorm didn't overlook this pertinent fact. When the room became available for students, almost everyone applied. The lucky winners, based on greatest combined seniority, were Chuck and Dave.

It was a small school with only twenty-three boys in the dormitory. Each night, five minutes after the dean had turned off the lights and retired to his apartment, twenty-two of the boys assembled in Chuck and Dave's room.

What did we do? Mostly we just sat around and talked, which we could have done just as easily in the darkness of any room. But this room was different because there was a lamp plugged into the closet and shedding its light to the whole room.

It was an exciting feeling just to look at that brightly shining lamp and know we were getting away with something that was against the rules. We were staring at an all-night light in a dormitory room!

Only one person was missing each night—Elmo. Elmo didn't want to be with us, and we didn't want him. Elmo didn't fit in.

The term "nerd" had not yet come into existence, but the characteristic of "nerdness" certainly had. Elmo didn't want to be like the rest of us. We didn't want to be like him. He was probably too naïve even to realize the presence of all-night lights in Chuck and Dave's room. Elmo lived by himself in a room near the opposite end of the first floor hall from Chuck and Dave. His room was immediately across the hall from the one Larry and I occupied. Nobody wanted to room with Elmo, and that was just fine with him.

One night as we sat around the brightly shining lamp in Chuck and Dave's room, I asked the guys, "How would you like to have all-night lights in every room in the dormitory?"

"Dream on," laughed Rick.

"No," I said. "I can make it happen. I've figured it out."

"How?"

"I'll rig up a special extension cord, plug one end into this live plug here in this closet, then plug the other end into the dead plug in the wall where the dean has turned off the current. The electricity will then back up through the circuit which has been cut off and supply current to every room."

"You're crazy," was the general response. "You don't know what you're talking about."

Someone else asked, "Have you ever fooled around with electricity?"

"No," I replied. "But I've got it figured out. It will work."

The guys were not exactly long on tact when expressing doubts. They gave me a very hard time. I would have to show them.

"Be here tomorrow night," I said. "five minutes after lights are out. I'm going to make believers out of all of you."

The next afternoon I went to town. I bought ten feet of extension cord wire and two male plugs. I wired plugs on each end of the cord. That night, five minutes after lights were out, I made my entrance to a room full of doubters. As usual, everyone was there except Elmo.

Trying to create as much of an atmosphere of

expectation as possible, I plugged one end of my apparatus into the live receptacle in the closet. I was ready to complete the task by plugging the other end into the wall when a thought stopped me dead in my tracks.

"Elmo" I groaned. "If Elmo's lights were on when the dean tripped the breaker, they will come on when I plug this in. He might tell on us."

Trying to maintain an air of being in charge and taking control of everything, I told the group, "I am personally going to go down the hall and stand outside Elmo's door. Sam, you take this cord; when I give the signal, plug it in. If I see light shining under Elmo's door, I will quickly open his door and turn it off. He'll never realize what has happened."

Handing the cord to a skeptical and reluctant Sam, I strode to the other end of the hall. Standing outside Elmo's room and staring down at the base of his door, I waved my hand as a signal for Sam to plug in the cord.

KER-POW!!! The entire building went dark! All the remaining lights went out instantly. Almost immediately, I heard the dean's apartment door open and his footsteps running up the stairs. I was standing in front of Elmo's door, just across the hall from my own room.

I dashed into my room, jumped into bed—shoes, clothes, and all—then pulled the covers over me up to my neck and closed my eyes. The rest of the guys didn't have a chance. With the dean's stairs leading right up to the room they were in, he was on them before even one had a chance to get away. With the aid of a flashlight, he took names.

Peeking out my door from under the covers, I could see the dean with his flashlight opening Elmo's door to check on him. He then proceeded to my room where he shined the light on me, eyes closed and apparently snoozing away.

Actually, there had been no electrical damage. The main breaker had tripped, and it had been a simple matter to reset it.

Normally, each morning we all assembled in the second floor assembly room for worship before going to breakfast. It usually took ten to fifteen minutes and consisted of a song, a talk or reading, and a prayer. The morning after the incident, the dean broke all records for worship brevity. He dispensed with the song, gave a two- or three-sentence talk, and barely started praying before he got to "Amen."

He then announced, "Elmo and Wayne can leave. The rest of you stay."

Elmo shrugged his shoulders quizzically, as he and I walked out of the room, as if to ask, "What's going on?" He then turned and headed for breakfast.

I stayed outside in the hallway after closing the double wooden doors to the worship room. I tried to look through the narrow slit where the doors came together. I couldn't see much.

Yet, I had no problem hearing. In no uncertain terms, the dean raked those guys up one side and down the other. As the party actually responsible, I felt very uncomfortable with the guff my friends were taking inside that room.

Then it got worse. The dean began to contrast their despicable natures with those of the two paragons of virtue, Elmo and Wayne.

That cut deeply. He was praising me, the guilty one, while condemning them, the innocent (or somewhat innocent) ones. Even worse, he was putting me into the same category as Elmo.

Finally he got to the punishment phase. Throwing the book at them, he socked them each with the boarding academy equivalent of the death penalty. Each was de-socialized for two weeks. Also, each was campus bound for two weeks. The sentences were to be served concurrently.

In a final vengeful gesture, he singled out Chuck and Dave as the suspected ringleaders of the episode. After all, it had happened in their room. Chuck and Dave were to be cast out of their beautiful home with the all-night lights and banished to the empty room next to Elmo. The offending room would be declared off limits and padlocked. This not only hit Chuck and Dave. Everyone lost the meeting place with its opportunity to bask in the glow of a clandestine lamp after 9:30.

All the guys were de-socialized and campus bound for two weeks—just because of me. They didn't deserve these atrocities—I did. But there I was, scot-free, while they suffered. A knot began to form in the pit of my stomach.

Suddenly, the dean dismissed them, the doors opened, and they began coming out. I wanted so badly to say something to them, but words just wouldn't come. Each one just silently glared at me as he filed past.

"Oh no," I thought. "How long will it be before someone goes to the dean and rats on me? Five minutes? Ten minutes?"

It didn't happen. No one told. Some enduring unwritten teenage code of honor dictates that you don't fink on another teenager no matter how deplorable the deed may have been, no matter how unjustly you are punished.

I was overwhelmed with gratitude. I felt immensely indebted to the guys. I would do anything I could do to relieve their suffering as they were crushed beneath the brutal weight of being de-socialized and campus bound. It was "Wayne Taylor, at your service. How may I help you? Do you need something from town? You've got it."

Actually, I had single-handedly shut down all social activity at the academy for two weeks. With the boys de-socialized, what could the girls do for dates? There were only two eligible bachelors left in the whole school—Elmo and me. Even if I had been more of a ladies' man, I wouldn't have taken advantage of the situation after what I had done to the guys. And no girl would be caught dead with Elmo.

You probably expect me to say that in my guilt-ridden state, I went to the dean and made a full confession. Yes, I did exactly that—two months later, on graduation day, after the commencement exercises, and with my diploma safely locked in the glove compartment of my parents' car.

I have been criticized, at times, for this delay in my confession, but the timing actually turned out to be just right. During the two months since the event, the dean had mellowed a lot. He had developed a sense of humor that had been in short supply the morning after the fiasco happened. We parted as friends.

Over the years, I have heard that our works don't save us, but rather that they should come as a natural response for what Christ did in dying for our sins—for His taking the punishment that we deserved so that we could be free. The concept of gratitude being the driving force for our actions is spelled out in 2 Corinthians 5:14, "The very spring of our actions is the love of Christ" (Phillips).

During the morning after the electrical incident, and during the two weeks that followed, I witnessed a somewhat crude, human glimpse of that concept. Innocent people were punished for my misdeed while I went free.

How much more we should be filled with gratitude for the sacrifice of the perfect, spotless Lamb of God! Those guys in the dorm were not perfect. They really shouldn't have been in Chuck and Dave's room after the lights were out. But they didn't deserve the retribution they received.

If I could feel so much gratitude for the fact that they took my punishment, I should feel infinitely more gratitude toward the sinless Jesus Christ who took my place on the cross.

> For He made Him who knew no sin to be sin for us, that we might become the righteousness of God in Him. (2 Corinthians 5:21, NKJV).

If our only response to Christ's sacrifice for our sins is to occasionally sing about it or to quote Ephesians 2:8, 9 in Sabbath School class, then maybe we haven't even begun to grasp the enormity of it. I might even be so brazen as to suggest that if the realization of Christ's sacrifice has not been the driving force in changing the way we act, perhaps we have not fully realized its magnitude.

The question is: Does the gratitude we feel compel us to change our actions?

CHAPTER 4

Potato Sandwiches

My first year of college was nearing its end. The natural question was: What was I going to do during the summer? I needed to earn some money to help with my expenses during the next school year.

Larry, my roommate from academy, contacted me. He was a year behind me in school, so my freshman year in college was his senior year in academy. Since we had been somewhat out of touch during the past year, he filled me in on his activities since my departure. He was full of glowing reports about his previous summer. He had gone to Cincinnati to stay with his older brother and had found summer work there.

"B-I-G money!" he exclaimed, extolling Cincinnati as a place where high-paying summer jobs were for the taking. He had done well, he said.

Before long, he had me convinced that Cincinnati was the promised land, the land flowing with milk and honey, the place some believe good people go when they die. I had never been to Cincinnati, but Larry painted a picture of a utopian paradise such as I had never seen.

He wasn't just talking to me. At the academy, he had been proclaiming Cincinnati's attributes to his friends. He had assembled a number of people who wanted to follow him to Cincinnati for the summer to make B-I-G money.

The only problem was that they wouldn't *exactly* be following him. Larry would be staying again with his older brother whose fraternal generosity did not quite extend to Larry's full circle of friends. However, Larry said that this shouldn't stop us from coming up on our own, getting a place to stay, and sharing expenses. After all, we were going to be making B-I-G money.

My parents were less enthusiastic about the idea than Larry was. They reminded me that Cincinnati was five hundred miles away and that I had never been there. If I wanted a summer job in a city, Memphis was less than an hour's drive away from home. In fact, several other cities were much closer both to home and to where I was going to college.

I had just turned nineteen. This made me the supreme authority on everything, and going to Cincinnati with my friends seemed perfectly logical to me. At last my parents caved in. I would be going with their blessing, albeit a rather reluctant blessing.

My dad even helped me get a car with the understanding that it was for the summer only and that it would have to be sold before school started. In those days, only a very few super-wealthy college students possessed cars at school, and I was not one of them.

The car was a 1939 Chevrolet, quite old even at that time. Yet, to me, it was the greatest car in the world because it was my car, at least temporarily. I would have the keys, and I would not have to ask to borrow the car. In this sense, it was my first real car.

Larry got in touch with me and told me that three of my friends from academy—Sam, Harry, and Eric—would be going to Cincinnati for the summer. All three had hoped to have cars, but things just didn't work out. I would be the only one with a vehicle. He suggested I contact Eric, who was taking care of details.

Eric told me that the three of them would be at camp meeting the next weekend. Since it would be right on my way to Cincinnati, I could pick them up, and we could drive on up. Eric had even located an Adventist lady, Mrs. Henderson, who had agreed—sight unseen—to rent us her basement apartment for the summer.

Soon we arrived in the Cincinnati area, located Mrs. Henderson and her basement apartment, and unloaded our belongings. We were ready to hit the streets with a fury the following morning and land those high-paying jobs.

We understood that the best-paying jobs were in factories, so I drove to an industrial area where we descended upon personnel offices. We had assumed that the four of us would be gobbled up together so we would all be working at one place.

It didn't take us long to realize that jobs didn't

come in fours. In fact, before long we weren't even
sure they came in ones. There was no sense in
the four of us competing with each other for the
few openings that existed.

So we spread out, dividing up the world each
day into our respective turf areas, each going out
alone. As the sole provider of wheels, this meant
I spent a lot of my time taking the guys to their
areas and picking them up. I also had to look for
my own job.

Before Friday of the first week, Harry had
become completely discouraged. Larry had convinced him that getting a job would be a piece of
cake. This clearly was not the case, so Harry said
Goodbye to us and went home.

Week number two found the remaining three
of us in the same routine. We had anticipated
being quickly employed, but we got no results
despite pounding a lot of pavement and pounding on a lot of doors. On Wednesday of the second
week, Sam gave up and went home.

Two days later, on Friday, at what seemed at
least my hundredth visit to a factory, I was hired.
I was told to report to work Monday morning at
a plant that made chrome plumbing fixtures for
bathrooms and kitchens.

On my way to pick up Eric, I couldn't wait to
tell him the good news. Maybe he had found something, too.

It was not the case. Eric was happy for me,
but he was heading for a real crisis. He was almost out of money, and there was no more where
that came from. Harry's and Sam's departures
had not bothered me that much. As I did, they
got some financial support from sacrificing par-

ents. Eric was different. He got no help. He was totally on his own. Probably for that reason, Eric was much more responsible than most guys I knew.

The next day at church, I discovered that a married couple, Lisa and Herman, also worked at the plant where I would be working. They passed near my apartment each day on their way to the job. They offered to pick me up and give me a ride every day without charging me anything. It was an offer I could not refuse. Since my commuting problem was solved, I told Eric to take my car and try really hard to get a job. He did try, but before the end of the week he couldn't continue.

"Wayne," he told me, "I'm sorry to leave you alone, but I'm flat broke. Thanks for letting me use your car, but I can't go on. I talked to Mrs. Henderson, and she agreed to reduce your rent so you won't have to pay what all four of us were planning to pay."

Eric left. I was alone. Should I leave, too?

Not on your life!

Leave? I had a job making a little more than the minimum wage, but still more than I had ever earned before. I had an apartment, although it would cost me more than I planned. I had friends my age in the local church. Most important of all, I had a car, a beautiful '39 Chevy.

To go home would be to admit failure. I had not failed; I had succeeded. The others may have failed, but I was sitting on top of the world, ready to enjoy a summer as an adult, totally on my own, totally self-sufficient. It wasn't depressing. It was exciting! I wouldn't be bored. For example, the annual church picnic was coming up. I was told that the other young people my age always had a lot of activities at the picnic. They could count on me to be there.

The picnic was on Sunday in the park. The park was in an extremely hilly area. There had been quite a bit of rain the day before, so the ground was soft and muddy. Driving into the park, I found all the paved parking areas taken. I had to park off the pavement, downhill from the road. As soon as I maneuvered into the place, I realized I would have a hard time getting out.

At the end of the day, when I tried to get my car up to the road, my wheels just sank deeper into the mud. I would back up, go forward, spin my wheels, and slide sideways. Finally, I managed to get out, but I had burned my clutch badly in the process.

Friends who knew about cars told me it wouldn't heal itself. It would just get worse. They were right. Within a few days the car would barely move. I was not enough of a mechanic to fix it myself. I would have to take it into a shop for repair.

It was Thursday afternoon. I took the car to a garage near my apartment and asked how much it would cost to fix the car. They looked at it and gave me a figure, telling me that if I left it that night, they could have it ready when I got home Friday afternoon.

The price disturbed me. It was almost the exact amount of the pay check I would be getting on Friday. I had just paid my rent and a few other expenses. I had no money left. There was almost no food in the apartment. It would be another whole week before I got paid again. I was counting on tomorrow's paycheck to live on for a week.

Yet, going a whole week without a car was a thought too horrible to contemplate. What should I do? An issue of this magnitude demanded resolution by scientific logic. In my mind, I outlined the pros and cons. To have a car for a week and starve, or to eat and be without wheels—that was the question.

These were the facts supporting one side:

- Lisa and Herman took me to work each day, so I didn't need the car to commute.
- If I had the car fixed now, I would have no money for food for a week.
- If I had the car fixed now, I would have no money for emergencies.
- I had no plans requiring a car for the upcoming week.
- Any stores where I needed to shop for food were within easy walking distance.
- If an emergency requiring transportation arose, Mrs. Henderson would take me.
- I needed to pay my tithe on my paycheck first, which would not leave enough to fix the car.

On the other side of the coin was just this one simple fact:

- I was nineteen years old.

Using the scientific method, made the answer perfectly clear. Given the facts marshaled above, the obvious, logical solution fairly screamed at me: I should spend the money to get the car fixed right away. I should "put first things first."

Anyone who has ever been nineteen years old understands that perfectly.

I left the car at the garage, told the mechanic to fix it and that I would be in the next afternoon to pick it up and pay him.

The next day I came home from work with pay in hand. I went directly to the repair garage where my wonderful 1939 Chevrolet was waiting. I paid for the repair job, receiving only a few small coins in change. I drove off, and the car performed magnificently.

Then reality began to set in. I went to the apartment and checked out my food supply. It consisted of a box of salt, a small amount of cooking oil in a bottle, and a partial loaf of bread with a total of eight slices—ten if I counted the two heels. That was all.

I felt the few small coins jingling in my pocket, afraid to count them. I scrounged around in empty pants pockets and under the cushion of the easy chair. Exhausting all sources of funds, I then audited my liquid assets—a grand total of thirty-three cents.

Thirty-three cents to live on for a full week! How would I live? Would I starve? I went to the supermarkets in the area with one thought in mind—to find the largest possible quantity of food of any kind that was available for thirty-three cents. Comparison shopping carefully, I found that one store had a special on potatoes—ten pounds for twenty-nine cents. I bought them. That left me with four cents.

Although those were days of much lower prices than today, I could not find any item selling for four cents. Even a candy bar cost a nickel. The ten-pound bag of potatoes looked pretty big. I thought it could last a week.

During the week that followed, I ate baked potatoes, boiled potatoes, mashed potatoes, fried potatoes, and some of my own creative potato recipes that I don't even care to remember.

I kept some boiled potatoes in the refrigerator, and every morning I would cut a few thick potato slices and put them between two slices of bread to make a potato sandwich. I would put the potato sandwich in my brown bag and take it to work with me for my lunch.

Normally, I brought my lunch and ate it in the area where the other employees ate theirs. This week, I went off into a remote corner to eat my potato sandwich. I was afraid someone would ask me what kind of sandwich I was eating.

Friday finally arrived. I put my last slices of boiled potato between my last two slices of bread. I went off into the corner to eat my last potato sandwich lunch. That afternoon, I picked up my paycheck and was financially solvent again. I never bit into another potato that entire summer.

Interestingly, I had not used my car all week.

This was one of life's little lessons on the subject of priorities. Priorities do not relate to what is good. They relate only to what is best among two or more alternatives that are all good.

When I was quite young, I was repeatedly exposed to those Bible stories that pitted the forces of good against the forces of evil. My religious education seemed to tell me that in real life, all choices would be between clear-cut good and clear-cut evil. I taught my own children the same way.

Reflecting on life, I now realize that most real-world choices relate to selecting the lesser of evils or the greater of goods. In and of itself, having a car is not intrinsically evil. It only becomes evil when it is given priority over a greater good.

In Mark 10:29, Jesus speaks favorably of people who have left brothers, sisters, parents, spouses, or children for His sake or for the sake of the gospel.

What? Those are some of the highest and most honorable relationships that exist among human beings. How can they be bad?

Even those relationships can be bad if they are not subordinated to what is most important. In the parable of the great supper (Luke 14:16-24), Jesus spoke of invited guests who declined to come to the supper for such reasons as recent purchases that needed to be checked out. He even told of newlyweds who understandably wanted to be together. These reasons for excusing themselves seem to be not only legitimate, but also very important.

The question is not what is important; it is what is *most* important. The term "prioritize" is not found in the Bible, but a good portion of the Bible is dedicated to the subject of prioritizing.

If you don't learn to prioritize, you could find yourself eating potato sandwiches.

CHAPTER 5

Blue Suede Shoes

College days were supposed to be happy days. Yet, there were times I felt a cloud of gloom settling in. This was not like me. I had to confront the problem. I had to analyze it. I had to find out what it was. Subjecting myself to deep introspection, I finally came to this disturbing self-diagnosis: I was suffering from severe deprivation of action with the chicks.

After the shock of this depressing realization set in, I did some intense soul-searching to determine its trigger mechanism. It was a struggle, but the basic cause of the problem finally emerged: I wasn't cool enough.

I knew a number of guys who were cool. They were fairly easy to identify. It was more difficult to dissect coolness; to isolate its component parts. I wanted to be cool, but how did I do it? Cool people seem to have been born cool.

The big question was: How do I become cool? The more I thought about it, the more convinced I was that coolness was an absolutely essential attribute that I must obtain if I was to have much involvement with females.

Becoming even more scientific in my approach, I theorized that coolness could be categorized into two branches. The first was coolness in the way a person acted and talked. The second was coolness in the way a person dressed.

The first involved personality. I had been struggling for years to develop a cooler personality, but without much success. This left the second aspect of coolness—relating to coolness in the way a person dressed. Even so, I still faced two barriers—money and taste. I didn't have enough money for a wardrobe of cool clothes, and even if I did, I didn't possess the knack of picking them out.

A light came on in my brain. Why not identify some single new style in one piece of apparel that was just beginning to come on the scene? Be one of the first to wear it. That should make me cool.

Tremendous idea! Now, what was just beginning to become popular that was pretty certain to become an "in" thing?

The answer came to mind swiftly—blue suede shoes! These particular items of apparel were already catching on quickly in most places, but very few people on my campus were sporting them yet. Here was my chance to catch the wave and ride in ahead of the crowd. Look out girls, here I come!

Blue suede shoes alone would not be enough. I wanted to carry it to a higher level. Soon half the guys on campus would be wearing blue suede shoes. I not only wanted blue suede shoes, I wanted blue suede shoes that would stand out in a crowd of other blue suede shoes.

Fortunately, I was able to scrounge up enough money to make a shopping trip into town. Many stores had blue suede shoes, but all the shoes looked pretty much alike. I was just about to conclude that if you have seen one blue suede shoe, you have seen them all.

I went into one last store. They immediately caught my eye—blue suede shoes that stood out from the rest! These shoes had white cotton stitching around the tops of the soles. This white stitching glistened in brilliant contrast to the deep blue suede. It took every penny in my pocket, but within minutes I was the proud owner of shoes that would undoubtedly make me the epitome of coolness.

Back on campus, I began to strut around in my blue suede shoes with white stitching. Rather than make any immediate overt moves in the area of socializing, I decided to first allow as many girls as possible to see me in the shoes. That way, they would all be after me and I could pick the cream of the crop. After all, now that I looked cool, I might as well play it cool.

I figured that three or four days of exposure should give most of the girls an opportunity to notice my shoes. Then I would make my move. Any girls who had not noticed my shoes by then would just be out of luck.

The first time I saw it was when I took my shoes off at the end of the second day. To my horror, I realized that the once-brilliant white stitching was turning a dingy gray!

The problem was that early in life I had developed the habit of wearing my shoes close to the ground. It gets dirty down there. There was no way to keep that dirt from invading the white stitching on my beautiful new shoes.

At this rate, something had to be done or my shoes would soon look just like the increasing number of other blue suede shoes that were beginning to appear on male feet all over the campus. I couldn't afford to lose my competitive edge.

Digging through a drawer, I found an old discarded toothbrush. Wetting and soaping it, I began to scrub the stitching vigorously. After about ten minutes of this activity, I held the shoes up to the light. My scrubbing with soap and water had transformed the dry dingy gray stitching into wet dingy gray stitching.

I tried using bathroom cleanser, but the results were no better. Laundry detergent bombed out too.

Then I saw a bottle of bleach. Now I knew I was getting into some heavier stuff that I might not understand, so I read the label. There were dilution directions for washing colors, for washing heavily soiled white clothes, and even for disinfecting. However, I could not find one thing on the label about whitening stitching on shoes. In the absence of anything specific, I fell back on an old scientific axiom to which I subscribed: "If a little is good, more is better."

Wetting the toothbrush in full strength bleach, I began to scrub again. Was it true? Could I believe my eyes? The gray of the stitching seemed to be getting lighter and brighter! I scrubbed harder, working more and more bleach down into the stitching. I could see progress!

The next morning, after the stitching dried

overnight, I looked at my shoes. The stitching was even lighter in color than the night before. I took a few minutes to give it another scrubbing with bleach before I left for class.

Throughout the day, whenever I had a break, I rushed back to my room to do another bleach scrub. By afternoon, the stitching was glistening as brilliantly white as ever before. Truly, I was being rewarded for my faith in the if-a-little-is-good-more-is-better principle.

Now I had learned that the price of keeping the stitching beautifully white was frequent brushing with full strength bleach. I did so at every opportunity. On one occasion I took extra time to really saturate the stitching in bleach, making me late for Dr. McKinley's class. The only seat left was immediately in front of the teacher.

Dr. McKinley began to sniff the air, and a worried look came over his face. "I think I smell a chlorine gas leak," he exclaimed. "I wonder if we should evacuate the classroom."

Finally he decided against it, and my shoes escaped being the reason for a dismissed class.

Several days passed. I was beginning to become concerned. The stitching on my shoes glowed a constant white from repeated bleach scrubbings, but the girls didn't seem to be paying much attention to me or my shoes. Had I been playing it too cool?

Maybe they just hadn't noticed. I needed to come up with a way to be sure they saw my shoes without making it too obvious.

In classes, I would strategically position myself by taking a chair between two girls. I would stretch one leg out straight with my heel on the floor and the toe of that foot pointing directly up. I would then straighten out my other leg, putting that heel on the toe of the first foot. With my two size-thirteen shoes sticking up in the air, one above the other, a total height of more than two feet was attained.

With two feet stacked vertically, I would gently sway them back and forth, pivoting on the lower heel. That way the white stitching of my blue suede shoes stood so high that it seemed impossible for the undulating movement to escape the girls' attention.

But apparently it did; there was no reaction from them at all. I could only conclude that when the girls in that college were in class, they were totally immersed in academic pursuits to the exclusion of all social distractions.

Perhaps it was time for me to make my move. There was no question as to the place to do so. The college cafeteria was in the basement of the girls' dormitory. To reach it, the guys would leave their dormitory and walk down a long sidewalk past the science building, past the administration building, and past the library to the stairs leading down to the cafeteria.

In front of the library were several park benches lining the sidewalk. Unoccupied most of the day, these benches would fill up with girls just before the evening meal when the guys would walk to the cafeteria.

These benches were "where it was at." This was where the chicks hung out. This was the place where the really cool guys would stop and talk with the girls, who seemed to lap it up.

I had tried to engage in conversation with

girls who were sitting on the benches, but without much success. Even if I did get the attention of one or two, it was short-lived, lasting only until one of the really cool guys moved in on me and captivated them.

To me, the benches represented the ultimate testing ground of establishing rapport with members of the opposite sex. This was where I had to succeed if I was going to be cool.

I planned my attack carefully. I took off a half hour early from work to have extra time to clean up and prepare. First, I bleach-scrubbed the already-white stitching on my blue suede shoes to give it a chance to dry before I got ready otherwise. I wanted the bleach smell to be gone before I put on the shoes.

Although I had shaved in the morning, I shaved again with a fresh blade. I showered, put on deodorant, brushed my teeth, then gargled and rinsed with mouthwash. I carefully combed my hair using Wildroot Cream Oil which at that time was considered the standard of men's hair care products.

Dressing was next, and I picked out my coolest wardrobe. Flowered shirts were in, if they were worn with light, solid-colored slacks. Argyle socks were the rage at that time. The bigger the argyle diamonds on the socks, the cooler. I had a pair that had only one diamond on each side, so big it occupied the entire side of the sock. They were a perfect match for my blue suede shoes with the brilliant white stitching.

A last glance in the mirror—I looked great. I smelled great. I felt great. This evening I was going to dazzle the girls on the benches. They would know that Wayne Taylor had arrived!

Nothing could stop me now.

All the other preparations and attire were important, but I knew that what set me apart was the blue suede shoes with the white stitching—the only pair on campus. Confidently, I strode down the sidewalk to the bench area.

Just as I got to the benches in front of the girls, I felt something that seemed to be on the bottom of the sole of one shoe, then the other.

"Oh no!" I thought, " I must have stepped on some chewing gum on the sidewalk. Don't look now; it wouldn't be cool to look at my shoes. I'll just step down hard and shift the soles of my feet back and forth until whatever it is comes loose."

Suddenly, right there in front of the girls, I got cold feet.

No, not cold feet in the figurative sense. I got cold feet in the literal sense. I realized that I was standing directly on the cold pavement with nothing between my feet and the concrete except my argyle socks.

This time I had to look down. To my dismay, the soles had come off both shoes and were lying on the sidewalk connected to my shoes by only a few remaining threads.

At that moment, I finally achieved something for the first time. I had the complete undivided attention of every girl on the benches.

Reaching down quickly, I gathered up the pieces of my shoes in my arms. Sock-footed and humiliated, I beat a hasty retreat down the sidewalk to my dormitory, accompanied by gales of laughter from the girls on the benches.

Nobody had told me that too much bleach, undiluted, would eat away cotton fibers such as made up the stitching that held the soles on my blue suede shoes. I had been so determined to make them look good on the outside that I was oblivious to the fact that it had come at a cost of all inner strength.

Outside, the stitching looked great. Inside, it was totally rotten. "Now do ye Pharisees make clean the outside of the cup and platter; but your inward part is full of ravening and wickedness" (Luke 11:39, KJV).

Self-righteousness is spiritual bleach. When we saturate ourselves with it, whom do we impress? God? Other people? Ourselves?

Not God, He certainly doesn't fall for it.

Other people? Maybe yes; maybe no. But we probably don't fool as many people as often as we think we do.

What about ourselves? This is the most dangerous game of all, because when we reach the point of totally convincing ourselves of the presumed merit of our own self-righteousness, we have put ourselves beyond the reach of the Holy Spirit. This is pushing very close to the unpardonable sin. In convincing ourselves of our self-righteousness, we fail at the very moment when we succeed. "All our righteousnesses are as filthy rags" (Isaiah 64:6, KJV).

Could we paraphrase that verse as "all our righteousnesses are as rotted threads?" Rotted inside by the self-righteous "bleach" we have applied so liberally to the outside, for the sake of appearance alone?

Bleach can cause you to lose your sole.

Self-righteousness can cause you to lose your soul.

CHAPTER 6

Night of the Chicken, Day of the Turkey

Thanksgiving break ended less than three weeks before Christmas vacation began. Considering the fifteen hours of travel required, I decided not to go home.

Although most of the students left, some stayed at school as I did. Wednesday night, Les invited Frank, Rusty, and me to his room just to sit around and talk. Boredom overwhelmed us around 10:30, so we went out into the dormitory hallway to see what was going on.

Nothing.

Nothing. Not a creature was stirring. The halls were deserted. Apparently, everyone who had stayed at school had already gone to bed.

"What's wrong with these guys?" questioned Frank. "Don't they realize that tomorrow is Thanksgiving? Nobody has to go to school. Nobody has to go to work. Why don't they stay up late, like us?"

Rusty chimed in, "There's nothing going on around here. We need some action to liven up this place. You don't go to bed early the night before turkey day."

Les and I agreed that it was too early to turn in, considering the holiday. The conversation continued to deteriorate into a discussion of how best to "strike a blow" at all the deadheads who had hit the sack early.

Various options were considered. Finally someone suggested, "Why don't we go out and round up some stray dogs and cats? Then we could open the doors of people we know are in bed, throw a dog or cat in on top of them, then close the door before they see who we are. That should put some life into the old dorm."

"Great idea!" everyone responded.

Why hadn't I thought of that?

Les and I enjoyed a prank as well as anyone. Yet, we were both thoroughly capable of enjoying it vicariously. In fact, we preferred that someone else do the dirty work and take the risk. This helped me maintain my unblemished record of never having been brought in on the carpet for any disciplinary matter either in academy or college.

Fortunately for Les and me, Frank had to be directly in on the action or it wasn't any fun for him. He seemed willing to get into almost anything. He was definitely a doer.

Rusty was Frank's protégée. To Rusty, Frank was his mentor and role model, especially when mischief was involved. He would blindly follow Frank into some of the craziest antics imaginable.

All this made it easy and convenient to divide up the responsibilities for this project. Frank and Rusty would go out and round up the dogs and cats while Les and I assumed the important role of staying in the dormitory and guarding the home front. As Frank and Rusty went out the front door to embark on their mission, I yelled after them, "Watch out for Virgil!"

Virgil was the school night watchman. He was an older student who was married. He owned a dilapidated car that he drove about the campus on his rounds, unlike other night watchmen who always walked.

The night watchman function existed solely because of a fire insurance requirement. The night watchman's only responsibilities were to report fires and to report burned-out light bulbs in street lamps. There was to be no law enforcement element to the position whatsoever. I know because all this was explained to me eighteen months later when I took the job as night watchman. Catching crooks was not part of the duties. I wouldn't have touched the job with a ten foot pole if it had been.

Yet Virgil envisioned himself a combination FBI Agent and U. S. Marshall in Dodge City. He probably harbored illusions of being a one-man SWAT team.

The school denied his request to carry a firearm. He had also asked for some kind of badge to enhance his image, but to no avail. Finally, using his own funds, he went out and bought a nightstick to carry as his symbol of authority.

In those days, violent crime was in rather short supply in that area. This seemed to frustrate Virgil. He needed some bad guys to apprehend in order to bolster his ego.

What did not exist in reality, Virgil apparently tried to concoct in his mind. The men's residence hall became his imagined hotbed of criminal activity. There was always a little tension—a little misunderstanding—between the married students and the single students. Single guys were Virgil's natural scapegoats. This made Frank and Rusty fair game for him—provided he could catch them.

Virgil or no Virgil, Frank and Rusty disappeared into the darkness. Les and I went back to his room to talk. At least forty-five minutes passed before Frank and Rusty returned. They were empty-handed.

"Couldn't find a single dog or cat," Frank reported.

"Or a married one either," wisecracked Rusty.

"Did Virgil catch you?" I asked.

"Naw," responded Rusty. "He's too dumb."

Despite the canine and feline shortage, Frank was not willing to give up. It was too good an idea. He had to find some animals somewhere.

"What about the farm?" Les suggested.

"A cow is too big to throw into somebody's bed. We'd never get one up here anyway," Frank objected.

The school had a farm which once had been quite extensive. Most of it had been shut down. Only a dairy herd remained.

"I think there are still some chickens down there," explained Les. "They are probably trying to get rid of them, but they seem to still be there."

"That ought to work," Frank said, his excitement starting to return. "Throw a chicken into somebody's bed, and he will come to attention fast. Come on Rusty, let's head for the farm!" They were gone in a flash.

About a half hour later, the door to the room flew open. Frank and Rusty ran in, panting and out of breath. "What's wrong?" Les wanted to know.

"Virgil!" was Frank's reply. "We were down there where they keep the chickens, and Virgil came in. He chased us all over the place before we finally got away."

"Did he see who you were?" I asked.

Rusty shook his head. "I don't know. Maybe so, but I hope not."

Just at that moment, there was a knock at the door. Who could be knocking at 1:00 A.M.? Frank opened the door.

Our hearts dropped to the floor. It was Virgil!

Fearing they had been had, Frank and Rusty were pale as sheets.

Virgil spoke, "I'm sorry to bother you fellows, but this was the only room with the light on. I need your help."

He looked around before continuing. "There are two chicken thieves on the loose out there, but I can't catch them by myself. Would a couple of you be willing to go out with me to try to find these chicken thieves?"

Frank and Rusty eagerly volunteered to accompany Virgil as his deputies in his quest to apprehend the poultry bandits. Wearing sly grins, they left with him. After a few chuckles with Les over the situation, I went to my room to go to bed.

Frank and Rusty told us the rest of the story

Thanksgiving afternoon. They had ridden around with Virgil in his car all night. From time to time, they would tell him that they thought they saw somebody. Virgil would then grab his trusty night-stick and give chase, sometimes crawling through underbrush, sometimes high-stepping through the barnyard where the cows congregated.

He never caught anyone. He never realized that the culprits were right there with him, in the form of his supposed allies. He had taken his enemies to be his partners.

Eve, too, thought she had found a new friend she could trust. He turned out to be a snake-in-the-grass (perhaps really a snake-in-the-tree, but you get the point).

Satan is the ultimate chicken thief, but that is only an incidental sideline with him. His specialty is stealing crowns. "Don't let anybody take your crown," (Revelation 3:11, Beck).

Will Satan take yours? You have one waiting for you (see 2 Timothy 4:8), but you can be duped out of it if you allow yourself to think your arch-enemy is really your friend. Satan doesn't do much parading around in a red suit with a pitch-fork and horns. His stock in trade is deceit. And no wonder, for even Satan "disguises himself as an angel of light" (2 Corinthians 11:14, RSV).

Is the "angel of light" you are responding to actually for real? You can blindly follow the ultimate chicken thief as he leads you on a wild chase through the dark of this world's night. Yet, when the day dawns—the day intended for giving thanks for wonderful blessings—you will find that you have missed the mark and come short of every goal.

CHAPTER 7

Reversed Vision and the King of the Disciples

During my college career, I spent a summer working as a student literature evangelist. A number of my fellow students were engaged in this occupation as well. But while other students were out setting records as rookie student literature evangelists, I was experiencing somewhat different results.

Before I began my summer of canvassing, I sought the advice of my father who, when he was in school, had also responded to the appeal to be a student colporteur.

"I think you should try it," he suggested. "I believe you will learn a very important lesson. I certainly did."

When I returned home briefly at the end of the summer, his first question was, "Well, what kind of lesson did you learn?"

"I learned never to try that again," was my instant reply.

"That's the same lesson I learned," he responded.

During the three months that had transpired between those two conversations, I had some interesting experiences. I could probably have contributed some colporteur rally stories, and I definitely saw the Lord leading and protecting in special ways in spite of my inept selling efforts. For example, there was my encounter with the pack of unfriendly dogs. Normally, dogs didn't bother me too much because I realized that most of them tend to bark at strangers, even student literature evangelists. This time however, the canines appeared to have fire in their eyes and mayhem in their hearts. The tactics of standing my ground and saying "nice doggies" was not paying off, indicating that they were not inclined to negotiate a peaceful settlement.

The dogs were between me and my car, and they were closing in fast. The only possible haven of refuge was a house that I had originally decided to pass up because it appeared too upscale. I ran for the front door.

With the dogs snarling at my heels, I bounded onto the front porch. At that moment, the door opened and a lady waved me in, slamming it in the faces of the pooches. I breathed a sigh of relief. That one had been close.

The lady invited me to sit down in a big easy chair and asked if I would like some lemonade. It was a very hot day, and her house was air conditioned—a rarity in that day and age. The refuge from the dogs, the comfortable chair, the lemonade, the cool relief from the heat, and the lady's kindness all made me feel so much at home that I wanted to stay.

This lady was so nice to me. What could I do to repay her kindness? The best thing I could think of would be to spare her from having to listen to my sales pitch. My canvass had not netted me one sale for over a week, so why burden her with it?

She complicated my benevolent intentions, however, by asking, "Why are you visiting in our area?"

"I'm selling books," I responded, "but they aren't anything you would be interested in."

"How do you know?" she asked. "Do you mind if I look?"

"Not at all," I replied, handing her my briefcase. "Help yourself."

While she looked through my case, I leaned back in the easy chair and closed my eyes, luxuriating in the atmosphere of my surroundings. After a considerable period of time, she tapped me on the shoulder to arouse me from my blissful half-slumber.

"Have I filled this out correctly and is this the right amount of money?" she asked as she handed me the completed order form and a handful of cash.

She had looked through my prospectus on her own and had read the price list and instructions for filling out the form. I was flabbergasted. She then showed me several other books she had obviously purchased from literature evangelists over the years. She said she enjoyed those books so much that she was looking for more.

A pack of angry dogs had chased me into a house that I didn't intend to visit. I had deliberately refrained from trying to sell anything. Yet I walked away with the full cash payment for what turned out to be my largest sale of the summer.

Although her cordial nature prevailed among her neighbors, this lady's genteel refinement was not very typical of the general populace of the vicinity. It was basically a rural area inhabited by people who were long on friendliness and deep-seated values, but a bit short on cultural breeding and educational sophistication.

It turned out that I didn't have exclusive selling rights for religious books in this territory. Although I never actually ran into him, someone else was going door to door in that same neighborhood selling modern language Bibles. In the mid-1950s, contemporary English versions were not playing all that well even with urbane urban Christians. Trying to sell them in this backwoods conservative piece of the Bible belt seemed almost suicidal. From the buzz of comments our common customer base made to me, it was clear that my competitor was definitely swimming upstream trying to sell that "new Bible."

I learned quickly to differentiate between the "new Bible" and my product, the *Golden Treasury of Bible Stories.* Although I refused to criticize the new version, early in my sales pitch I would make sure to get in the comment that all the stories in the *Golden Treasury* are found in the King James Version. I didn't mention the fact that the same stories are also found in modern language versions. I was just trying to defuse the bias, and it usually worked.

Reversed Vision and the King of the Disciples

My encounter with Rufus was fairly typical. I knocked at his door, exchanged a few pleasantries, and began pulling my prospectus from the case while I was talking.

"That ain't thet thar new Bible, is it?" Rufus asked, cutting me off in mid-sentence.

"No, Sir," I assured him, adding my usual comment about all these stories being found in the King James Version. In my heart I wanted so badly to enlighten the man and to come to the defense of modern language versions. Yet, I realized that to do so would undermine my efforts and, in his mind, discredit everything I would say.

"I don't want to have nothin' to do with that reversed vision of the Bible," Rufus continued emphatically.

"*Revised version,* Rufus, not *reversed vision,* " I said to myself, not daring to correct him audibly. Obviously, Rufus was the one with reversed vision.

He picked up his well-worn Bible from the table and waved it in the air. "See this?" he demanded. "This here is the only Bible I have and the only one I need. It's the good ole King James Bible, the one written by James, who was one of the twelve disciples. They called him King James because he wrote the Bible."

Rufus obviously possessed a wealth of ignorance, bordering on gross stupidity. I was sorely tempted to set him straight in no uncertain terms, but I managed to resist the urge. I would be wasting both time and friendship trying to tell him that King James was actually James I of England who commissioned the Authorized Version to be translated from the oldest and most reliable manuscripts available in the early 1600s—not the James who was one of the twelve disciples of Jesus.

And speaking of James the disciple, which one, Rufus? Two of the twelve disciples were named James. There was James, the son of Zebedee, brother of John, and one of the "sons of thunder." He was one of the close inner circle of three who accompanied Jesus to places like the top of the Mount of Transfiguration and the deeper recesses of the Garden of Gethsemane.

Then there was also James, the son of Alphaeus, specifically identified four times in the Bible as one of the twelve disciples. However, it is unlikely that either of these men wrote one word of the Bible. According to most experts, the New Testament book of James was written by James, the brother of the Lord. This James was one of the four original sons of Joseph, Jesus' earthly father. This James was a disciple only in the broadest sense. He was not one of the twelve.

Now, my Bible knowledge is very mediocre compared with legitimate theologians. Yet when I think about how dumb Rufus was and begin to compare my Bible smarts with his, my chest begins to swell with pride. Unlike Rufus, I have an open mind on new Bible translations. At last count I had twenty-three different versions of the Bible on my shelves. In addition, my personal library includes a huge collection of Spirit of Prophecy volumes, numerous concordances, commentaries, and reference works—many hundreds of religious books in all. "Try to match that, Rufus!"

All these resources make the challenge of

Bible study even more enjoyable. As a Sabbath School teacher, my favorite quarterlies are those that take an entire book of the Bible and follow it through from the first verse to the last. In doing this, there is no way to avoid difficult texts. There are three ways, all cop-outs, that many people use in dealing with difficult texts.

The first approach that some use is to say that God doesn't want us to understand some things, at least in this life. I agree that God doesn't want us to understand some things now, but those things do not include Bible texts. *All* Scripture is inspired by God (see 2 Timothy 3: 16, RSV). "For whatsoever things were written aforetime were written for our learning, that we through patience and comfort of the scriptures might have hope" (Romans 15:4, KJV). Of course, we need the Holy Spirit's guidance, but a text would not be in the Bible if it were not to be understood. We criticize those who say that Revelation is a closed book. The Bible has neither closed books nor closed texts.

Another faulty approach in dealing with a problem text is to immediately find other texts to refute it. Bible truth is not based on the "majority rule," on lining up more texts that seem to say one thing versus a fewer number of texts that seem to say the opposite. Inspired searching of the Scriptures will lead us to an understanding of the problem text, and we will discover that it is not in conflict with other texts. Individual books of the Bible were written by many people from various cultures over more than a thousand years. One of the many evidences of the Bible's divine inspiration is the fact that it does not contradict itself—it has harmony.

A third way of handling problem texts is simply to ignore them, saying, "A close walk with Jesus Christ is the most important thing, so I try to stay away from doctrine. I leave that to the theologians."

What is doctrine, other than the revelation of God's will for our lives? How can we say that we want to have a close walk with Jesus Christ if we couldn't care less about how He would like for us to respond? We need to learn for ourselves. If we accept the Protestant principle of the priesthood of all believers, each of us is ultimately our own theologian.

With this challenge, how can I face the text without all the resources that I can accumulate?

Thus, my various versions of the Bible make me much more comfortable. But as I bask and wallow in this cozy pride, my comfort is suddenly shattered by these questions: Has all this doctrine—all this revelation of God's will for my life—made me a better person? How much have I grown spiritually since my encounter with Rufus more than four decades ago? Have all these literary resources left me with a closer relationship with God than the relationship Rufus, with his one King James Bible, had?

"Every one to whom much is given, of him will much be required" (Luke 12: 48, RSV).

CHAPTER 8

A Bad Stroke at the Driving Range

Long before I graduated from college, the fighting had stopped in Korea. No one was sure the cease-fire would last, but there was no more shooting of any significance. Even so, Korea was not a place I really wanted to go. Almost instinctively, I enrolled in a master's degree program at a nearby university. If I stayed in school long enough, maybe my draft board would lose my file.

Not a chance. After one term in graduate school, I received my "greetings," a notice from the draft board to report for duty. I quickly reminded the members of the board that they had said they would defer me as long as I attended school. They replied that my new school had never notified them that I was a student and that they would be happy to continue my deferment as soon as they got such a notice.

Assessing the situation and being honest with myself, I made several observations. I was tired of playing games with the draft board. I was tired of not earning enough money even to cover my school expenses. Frankly, I was also tired of going to school. The inevitable was inevitable.

Going back to the draft board, I inquired, "No matter how long I stay in school, you are going to get me in the end, aren't you?"

"You can run, but you can't hide," was the reply.

"Then forget the deferment," I said. "Take me. I'm yours."

Several weeks later, the day came to report for duty. My parents, my sister, and my brother assembled with me in the living room for a farewell.

Somewhat to my surprise, my Uncle Darrell came over. Uncle Darrell never said much, but I appreciated the fact that he came because he had served in the army for four years during World War II. Before the war, Uncle Darrell had been a good automobile mechanic. In its great wisdom, the army made him a cook. However, he represented the voice of military experience, although his voice almost never spoke.

In the midst of all the tearful goodbyes, a hush fell over the room. Uncle Darrell was about to say something! This had to be something really important.

Four words issued from Uncle Darrell's lips: "Never volunteer for anything."

"Never volunteer for anything." This was the accumulated wisdom from his four years of military service. Those words seemed important. I would remember Uncle Darrell's counsel.

A few days later, I began basic training at Fort Sam Houston, Texas. Basic training was not what I had expected. I had thought we would go through a tough fitness regimen that would whip our bodies into shape.

Not so. Other than a little marching around, almost all our time was spent sitting down, either in outdoor bleachers or indoor classrooms. We had to listen to dry boring lectures, doing our best to stay awake.

But about once every two weeks, for half a day, it happened.

The company clerk—a guy who sat behind a typewriter all day—was small, thin, and bespectacled. He was also an Adventist. I thought that would make him gentle and considerate, especially with his fellow brethren.

Wrong! Little did I know that he was a physical fitness nut who constantly worked out, pumped iron, and ran long distances. He fervently believed in sharing his physical fitness faith with all the namby-pamby recruits that he felt needed it so badly.

Twice a month, he was granted custody of us for a few hours. To set the stage, he would drop to the ground and do a hundred one-arm pushups—first right-handed, then left-handed. Then he would put us through our paces doing physical training exercises such as I had never seen before. In less than ten minutes, even the toughest recruits would be lying on the ground, out of breath, their muscles wracked with pain. Two sedentary weeks with no exercise can mess up even guys who had previously been in good shape. The company clerk was merciless, and he forced us to keep going even beyond the limit of human endurance.

This ordeal would be followed by another fortnight of almost complete physical inactivity before he would be turned loose to brutalize us again.

One Friday, our drill sergeant announced, "Next week we will spend all five days at the driving range."

"All day, every day, Sarge?" someone asked.

"All day, every day," he answered.

To me, that was wonderful news! I was a fledgling golfer, and I had been to a driving range several times. Forty hours at the driving range ought to add distance to my tee shots and also straighten out my hooks and slices.

There were several other golfers in our barracks. They were also happy and eager for Monday morning to come.

"Whoa!" you are probably saying. "Five days at the driving range hitting golf balls? As a part of army basic training? That doesn't make sense."

Of course it doesn't make sense. Almost nothing about basic training made sense. Not making sense was normal. If anything made sense, we would think something was wrong. After all, our leaders had taken us out to a field to play softball one afternoon. They had us play volleyball several times. There was a basketball goal where we shot hoops. Why not golf?

On Monday morning we went to an open area out in the boonies. Other than a lot of Army trucks, there was nothing to be seen except the rutted, scraggly field, parched dry by the south

Texas sun. This was unusual. Every driving range I had seen had nice green grass that was kept mowed.

Not to worry, I thought. The balls would bounce farther on the hard, baked ground, adding distance to my drives. This was just typical military austerity. Probably the clubs would be olive drab and the balls khaki colored. The trucks were probably carrying the clubs, the tees, the balls, and the ball retrieval equipment. I didn't understand why there were so many trucks though.

The sergeant spoke, "Welcome to the driving range, men. You are going to learn to drive. You are going to learn to drive these trucks. Most of you think you already know how to drive, but you know only how to drive like a civilian. We are going to teach you how to drive the army way."

Well, so much for golf! Anyway, racing around these fields in a truck would probably beat sitting in bleachers and classrooms all day. I was prepared to make the best of it.

The sergeant explained the ground rules. We were to drive these trucks around the perimeter of the field at four miles an hour. We were to make a rounded left turn at each of the four corners of the field. We were to maintain a constant equal distance between trucks so that at all times the trucks made an unbroken continuum all around the field. There must never be any deviation.

Two people were assigned to each truck, a driver and a passenger. One person was to drive for two hours, while the other occupied the passenger seat. The pair would then trade off for the next two hours.

Around and around the perimeter of the field we went, bouncing over bumpy ruts left by others who had gone before us. As directed, we carefully maintained equal distance between trucks as we inched along at the agonizing snail's pace of four miles an hour.

Talk about boredom—this was worse than the classrooms! It was the same thing over and over. We became so familiar with the route that we knew which bump was coming next. To relieve the agonizing sameness, we developed a kind of game in which the driver would close his eyes and follow the spoken directions of the passenger. After a while the bumps that we felt with our eyes closed became so familiar and predictable that even this game was no longer challenging.

We then modified the game to see if the driver could make it all the way around the field, maintaining proper distance, with both the driver's *and* the passenger's eyes closed, guided only by the familiarity of the bumps! Actually, at four miles an hour, this was not as daring as one might think.

Throughout the week, our drill sergeant mentioned several times that there would be an exhaustive driver's test on Friday afternoon. Those who passed would receive that most coveted prize—a military driver's license.

Day after day we went around that field, always the same. Hundreds of times I drove around it. Hundreds of times I rode around it in the passenger seat. It was a terribly long week, but Friday afternoon finally came. We got out of our trucks and lined up behind nine sergeants—an equal number of men in each line. These sergeants were from the motor pool, and they would be giving us our driving tests.

Only one of them had a friendly smiling face, so I jumped in line behind him. One by one, we were tested with the motor-pool sergeant in the passenger seat. Our test consisted of driving one time around the perimeter of the field at four miles an hour, just as we had done all through the week.

When it was over, we were each handed a slip of paper with our driver's test result. I looked at mine. There, stamped in big bold letters, was the word "FAILED."

Failed? How could that be? Had everybody failed? I asked around. Almost everyone else had passed. What was wrong? We all drove the course identically.

I was some kind of ticked off. A few others had failed, but not many. The guys who passed had a field day ribbing those few of us who had failed something so ridiculously simple.

As those of us who failed compared notes, one common thread emerged. We had all been tested by the same smiling motor pool sergeant. Checking further, we found that no one who had passed had been tested by him. We asked our drill sergeant about this. He laughed and explained that the motor pool people were being criticized for being too lenient and passing everyone who took the driver's test. So the motor-pool sergeants decided that they would maintain an 11 percent failure rate by taking turns as the designated failer. One sergeant would fail all the people he tested while the other eight would pass all they tested. It kept their statistics credible.

Not my idea of fairness, but who said the army was fair? What bothered me most was the damage to my male ego. In that more chauvinistic era, a person of my gender who couldn't even pass a driver's test was a real outcast.

After the first eight weeks of basic training at Fort Sam, we went into the second eight weeks at the same place. The second eight-week session was called medical basic. The medical was so basic that it was on about the level of a fifth- or sixth-grade health class. As an example, the course set aside three days to teach us how to read an ordinary fever thermometer.

The one incursion into "highly advanced" medicine was when we were taught how to give a hypodermic injection. Our instructors had us pair off in twos to inject each other. I wanted to team up with a medical clinician of some kind who had given shots to people before. There not being any, I paired off with a recruit who had been an undertaker, figuring his experience was better than none.

The good news was that we finished our second eight weeks of training, at last, and were ready for permanent assignment. The bad news was that we were told our assignment would be Korea—not my first choice as a destination, at least at that time.

We lined up in alphabetical order and started loading ourselves and our gear into two military aircraft that were to take us to Fort Lewis, Washington, the jumping-off place for Korea. The last fourteen—including me—would not fit on the planes.

Fourteen was too small a number to justify bringing in another military plane. So we were to go by commercial airline, which required that separate orders be cut for us. Cutting separate orders technically isolated us from the rest of our group.

Interestingly, while we fourteen were being processed at Fort Lewis, the main post dispensary developed a need for exactly fourteen people with medical basic training! Our end-of-the-alphabet group fit the need precisely, so they took us. Everybody else went to Korea.

We were ushered into a room at the main post dispensary, and a warrant officer interviewed us as a group. "How many of you know how to type?" was his first question.

"Of course I know how to type," I said to myself, remembering my experiences in typing classes. I started to raise my hand along with several others.

Then Uncle Darrell's sage advice rang in my ears—"Never volunteer for anything." My hand came down. Nobody had seen it. Whew!

"You people who raised your hands will be assigned clerical jobs. You will work eight hours a day, Monday through Friday."

"Not bad," I thought. "Almost like a civilian job. Maybe I should have raised my hand."

"How many of you know how to give injections?" was the next question.

Several people began slowly raising their hands. I was struggling in my mind whether I should raise mine. We had each given one injection during training. I was just as poorly qualified as anyone else. Finally, Uncle Darrell's words of wisdom prevailed. I kept my hand down.

The warrant officer stated, "You people who raised your hands will be assigned as medical corpsmen to assist in the clinic and to attend to patients on ambulance runs. You will alternate with others in eight-hour shifts, totaling forty hours a week."

"Still not too bad," I mused. "It gives a little flexibility."

The warrant officer looked at those of us who were left. "The rest of you must not know how to do anything. You will be assigned as ambulance drivers. You will be on call for twenty-four hours, then off duty for seventy-two hours. When you are on call, you must stay nearby within reach, but you may sleep, watch television, read, or do anything else as long as it does not take you away from here. All our ambulance runs are emergencies only. When you are off duty, your time is your own."

"Thank you, Uncle Darrell!" I breathed a sigh of relief. By not raising my hand, I had landed the cushiest job of all.

The warrant officer's next question jolted me back to reality. "How many of you hold a military driver's license?"

Every hand went up except mine. This time I wanted so badly to raise my hand, but I couldn't. The friendly, smiling motor-pool sergeant in Texas had done me in.

What would happen? "He thinks I can't type. He thinks I can't give shots. Will I be sent to Korea after all?

The warrant officer spoke again. "Sergeant, take this man down to the motor pool and get him a military driver's license."

Some relief began to emerge. As I rode with the sergeant down to the motor pool, questions began popping into my mind. Would I have to drive a truck around a field at four miles an hour for a week? What if I once again line up behind the wrong tester?

We went into the office of a motor-pool sergeant. My sergeant told him I needed a driver's license. He took down my name, rank, serial number, and date of birth. He then began filling out a form, but I couldn't tell what it was. He filled out a second form, popped a small card into a typewriter, and typed something on it.

When he finished, he handed it to me. "This is your military driver's license," he said, "You do know how to drive, don't you?"

"Of course," I responded, hardly believing what was happening.

"Good," he said. "That's all there is to it."

Curious, I asked, "What were those two forms?"

"Oh," he replied, "the first was your written test; I filled it out for you. The second was your driving test. I answered a couple of questions wrong on the written test because people become suspicious about perfect scores. For the same reason, I dinged you on the driving test for failure to look before you backed up. Both scores leave you well within the passing range."

I left in happy bewilderment. The same type of bureaucratic farce that previously had failed me unjustly, had now passed me unjustly.

Do two wrongs make a right? Probably not, but I knew I could drive, and I knew that I could pass both the written and the driving tests if they were fairly administered. I had my license. My macho image was restored.

I had gone around in circles for a week. Then I lined up behind someone who seemed to be friendly and smiling—and I totally bombed out. I had been set up.

After that, I went to someone else who took my test for me. Going to him, it was a sure thing that I would pass without going around in circles and without effort on my part.

Life is a test. If you line up behind Satan because he appears to be smiling and friendly, he will send you around in circles continuously. In the end, you will fail miserably. "To whom ye yield yourselves servants to obey, his servants ye are to whom ye obey" (Romans 6:16, KJV).

Instead, go to Jesus Christ. He has already taken your test for you, and if you just go to Him to receive it, He will give you your license to salvation. "Thanks be to God, who gives us the victory, through our Lord Jesus Christ" (1 Corinthians 15:57, RSV).

CHAPTER 9

The Mega-Bite Denture Adventure

My two-year army tour would soon end. It had been an interesting experience, to say the least.

Growing up during World War II, I had heard countless stories of Adventists who had been drafted into the military and whose faith had been severely tested. Some had faced almost inhuman treatment for standing up for their beliefs. This was one reason I had feared the draft so much. In academy I took Medical Cadet Corps training to prepare me and to steel me for the upcoming ordeal.

To my surprise and relief, the ordeal never materialized. Basic training in the army was not nearly as rigorous or demanding as the Medical Cadet Corps had been. I never had to work up the courage to go in to ask my commanding officer for the Sabbath off. At the very beginning, we were told that Sabbath passes would automatically be handed out to all Seventh-day Adventists each Friday before sundown.

When I was assigned to the main post dispensary to drive an ambulance, I found that being an Adventist actually meant red-carpet treatment and special privileges. The officers explained that this was because they had never had an Adventist ever let them down regarding any responsibility or assignment. They had not had that experience with any other identifiable group—religious or otherwise.

Almost half of my medic group were Adventists. Together, we immediately recognized that we owed a tremendous debt of gratitude to scores of Adventists who had gone before us. And we were determined to repay that debt by leaving an equal, or even more favorable, impression from which those who came after us could benefit.

As a people, perhaps we Adventists would not face nearly as much difficulty if we went out of our way to be cooperative—not only to impress people with our helpfulness, but to *be* helpful and to be certain that they associate the cause with our being Adventists. In our paranoia, we bemoan the fact that we are sometimes the victims of adverse stereotyping. But if we conduct ourselves as responsible, caring Christians, it can work the other way. God expects each of us to be a "spectacle to the world, to angels and to men." (1 Corinthians 4:9 RSV).

As medics, we made a lot of friends, particularly with certain groups. One such group was the Military Police, or MPs. A symbiotic relationship naturally develops between ambulance crews and police because they work closely together in so many emergencies.

Around military installations, it is normal for emergency-services people, such as MPs or ambulance crews, to stay quite busy on Saturday nights. On weekday nights, especially after midnight, things can become rather dull. At such times, usually the only people who are awake and on duty are the MPs and the medics at the main post dispensary. Since no doughnut shops were open during the wee hours, the night patrol MPs would drop by the dispensary to take their breaks and talk.

As we sat around, we would recount situations in which both MPs and ambulance medics had been involved. We medics would tell the MPs some of our ambulance adventures, to which they would respond with some of their police tales.

One ongoing saga that the MPs continuously updated us on involved a married couple who got drunk and ended up fighting every Saturday night. The woman was two or three times the size of the man, so she always got the best of him and usually beat him up. He had never required medical attention from us, but the MPs assured us that it would be only a matter of time before he would.

There are far too many tragic cases of physical spousal abuse. In the great majority of cases, it is the wife who is the victim. This situation was the exception, with the husband being the one who was mauled. Although this story has its humorous elements, I'm far from suggesting that spouse abuse is not a serious issue.

One Saturday night we finally got the call. An MP was on the phone. "This is your chance to see what we have been talking about," he said. "The man is really beat up this time; he needs a lot of stitches on his head. Hop into the ambulance and come on over." He gave us the address of the apartment, and we were on our way.

When we arrived, we found both husband and wife significantly inebriated. They had been fighting, apparently with their clothes off, but the MPs had put a blanket around each of them. Their intoxication made it impossible for them even to dress themselves.

Just as the MPs had told us, the man was short and scrawny. He couldn't have weighed more than a hundred pounds soaking wet. He was also totally bald—bald as the proverbial billiard ball.

In contrast, the woman towered far more than six feet tall. She was also quite heavy; to put it bluntly, she was downright fat. There just isn't any other way to put it. She was indeed a massive woman in every respect—not one you would want to encounter on unfriendly terms in a dark alley.

The man's face was battered and bruised; one eye was swollen shut. However, his most immediate problem was a severely lacerated scalp on top of his bald head.

In their tussle, his missus had applied her chompers to the top of his head in a rather vigorous manner. She left a roughly round piece of scalp, about two inches in diameter, dangling by little more than a thread. There were other teeth marks in his bald pate. I reasoned that they must have been inflicted by his wife, as it would have been somewhat difficult for him to have bitten himself in those particular spots.

The lady had false teeth. Apparently in the process of incising the chunk of her husband's scalp, her dentures had come loose and fallen out. Polygrip may be effective for biting into apples and corn on the cob, but it makes no claim for effectiveness when biting bald heads.

While we were looking at the man's injuries, the lady was vociferously lamenting the loss of her dentures. "Where are my teeth? I can't find my teeth. Who has my teeth? Help me look for my teeth," she exclaimed over and over in her drunken state.

It was obvious that the man should be seen by a doctor. A human bite can be very serious, even if inflicted by a devoted spouse. A considerable amount of suturing would also be required. We got the man into the ambulance.

One of the MPs told the woman that she should go too. She protested, "I'm not going anywhere without my teeth!"

We all looked around for her teeth, but to no avail. And she refused to go without them. She also refused to go to her bedroom and get dressed. She just stood there defiantly, clad in a large blanket. Finally, an MP said, "Look lady, you don't have any choice. I am placing you under arrest for refusing to cooperate with a military police officer."

After a lot of pushing, pulling, shoving, and yelling, we finally got the lady into the ambulance with her husband. All the while she was loudly protesting being forced to leave home without her teeth. An MP sat on each side of her in the ambulance to protect her husband from any further violence.

At the dispensary, we all went to the clinic area with the lady constantly grumbling about the loss of her teeth. The doctor looked at the bite on the man's head and asked for some help in preparing medication and suturing necessities.

While we were preoccupied, someone noticed that the lady had disappeared. "We had better go and find her," an MP said. "She's drunk as a skunk."

Several of us fanned out in different directions. I took the hallway that led to the front of the building where the ambulances were parked. About halfway down the hall, I came across the blanket she had been wearing. I picked it up and went outside.

There I found her, sitting on the back bumper of the ambulance in her birthday suit. I tried to put the blanket back around her the best I could. She refused to budge.

"We need to go inside," I said. "It's cold out here."

She retorted angrily, "I'll have you know that I'm a lady, and a lady never goes anywhere without her teeth!"

That lady clearly did not understand what was important. She was so obsessed with wanting teeth that she was oblivious to the fact that her greatest need was clothing. More than anything else, she needed to be robed.

In the Laodicean condition that so often grips us, we tend to be the same way. What we need more than anything else is to be dressed in the robe of Christ's righteousness. Yet, all we seem to want to focus upon is teeth—teeth that bite, teeth that can inflict pain upon people who don't see things our way. We want teeth—sharp teeth representing power, authority, and control.

That is not God's way. "Not by might, nor by power, but by my Spirit saith the Lord of hosts" (Zechariah 4:6, KJV).

What we need, what we want, and what we think we have can be confusing. The message to Laodicea includes:

For you say, I am rich, I have prospered, and I need nothing; not knowing that you are wretched, pitiable, poor, blind, and naked. Therefore I counsel you to buy from me gold refined by fire, that you may be rich, and white garments to clothe you, and to keep the shame of your nakedness from being seen (Revelation 3:17, 18 RSV).

White garments—the robe of Christ's righteousness. This is more important than all the teeth, all the might, and all the power that this world can offer.

If you enjoyed this book, you'll enjoy these as well:

Even the Angels Must Laugh Again
Jan S. Doward. A favorite collection of humorous stories back in print with new stories added! Each story is a reminder of the joy of being a Christian and the wonder of a God who created laughter.
0-8163-1408-X. Paperback. US$5.99, Cdn$8.49.

Growing Up Adventist
Andy Nash. Hilarious but meaningful stories about growing up in the church. Told with love and sprinkled with appreciation for the God who began and directs this movement.
0-8163-1365-2. Paperback. US$9.99, Cdn$14.99.

Order from your ABC by calling **1-800-765-6955,** or get online and shop our virtual store at **www.adventistbookcenter.com.**
- Read a chapter from your favorite book
- Order online
- Sign up for e-mail notices on new products